Seminar Marketing & Sales Training Techniques for the Financial Professional

WELCOME

TODAY'S AGENDA:

Seminar Marketing & Sales Training Techniques for the Financial Professional

Frank James Eberhart, CEP, RFC,
author of *Plan Ahead: Protect Your Estate and Investments*

iUniverse, Inc.
New York Lincoln Shanghai

Seminar Marketing & Sales Training Techniques
for the Financial Professional

Copyright © 2006 by Frank J. Eberhart

iUniverse books may be ordered through booksellers or by contacting:

iUniverse
2021 Pine Lake Road, Suite 100
Lincoln, NE 68512
www.iuniverse.com
1-800-Authors (1-800-288-4677)

ISBN-13: 978-0-595-37164-8 (pbk)
ISBN-13: 978-0-595-81563-0 (ebk)
ISBN-10: 0-595-37164-7 (pbk)
ISBN-10: 0-595-81563-4 (ebk)

Printed in the United States of America

To P & M; my wife, Jodi; daughters, Zoe and Kate; sons, Zak and Chris; and grandkids, Nick and Bailey.

CONTENTS

I. Introduction

Have you ever spent many hours and thousands of dollars to produce mailings and handouts, line up guest speakers, and make preparations for a seminar—just to have nobody show up? Or worse, have you ever conducted a seminar that had far more people presenting than sitting in the audience? Been there, done that.

Well, after trying just about everything, from using direct-mail companies—which often fail to get the type of response I'm looking for, and over whose list you have no control—to hiring professional printers, to stuffing envelopes and licking stamps, I've seen what does and doesn't work. I've even prepared seminars that cover dry, boring topics such as estate planning and financial planning (everybody was doing these, and nobody cared to much for them). In my experience, the following maxim always holds true: *No topics, no agenda, no response!*

Regardless of your profession, a well-organized seminar agenda that defines both your target audience and the main discussion topics results in better attendance, better expectations, and better results. Through this book, you will learn that running effective seminars is an art form of its own.

Specifically, *Seminar Marketing & Sales Training Techniques* will instruct you in the following areas:

- Proper marketing and targeting
- Proper topics and agendas
- Client-closing skills
- Seminar setup
- Presentation skills
- Proper handouts
- PowerPoint presentations
- Form creation

This book is designed primarily to assist those in the financial marketplace, but the principles can be adapted to any business that conducts seminars. It not only covers how to conduct a successful seminar but also discusses the five essential tools to use before, during, and after the seminar to help ensure your success.

I cannot stress enough the importance of *preparation, practice,* and *follow-up,* for each of these actions brings equally positive results.

I have kept this book short, direct, and to the point to prove the *effectiveness of simplicity.*

Have a successful seminar!

Frank J. Eberhart, CEP, RFC
(Over 90% of my clients have come from seminars!)

II. The Cart before the Horse

In today's marketplace, you must compete against thousands of other financial professionals, large brokerage houses, boutique firms, banks, accountants, and now, potentially, lawyers.

With all this competition, how do you obtain new clients?

New national and statewide do-not-call lists have made cold-calling a difficult option. Not all phone number lists are scrubbed, or checked, against these do-not-call registries, and violations of these lists carry an $11,000 fine per offense! Direct mailers usually garner very poor results. Referrals? I find that high-net-worth clients do not like to give referrals. They say, "Now my neighbor knows what I'm worth," and "My neighbor is my friend, and if the referral doesn't work out, I still have to live by my neighbor and may have lost a friend." Chamber of Commerce events and workshops may provide other avenues of gaining new clientele.

However, the best way to obtain clients, in my opinion, is through seminars.

Seminars provide you with a voluntary, captive audience that wants to understand what you and your firm have to offer, and you generally have around one and a half to two hours to convince them to do business with you.

How long do you think it might take you to find thirty-five to forty high-net-worth clients at one time to sit in front of you for two hours? You may never get that many high-net-worth clients, or it may take years to find them.

Individuals who attend seminars do so by choice and are responding to a particular need they are trying to fulfill. (They are either trying to confirm that they made a good choice or are unhappy and looking for a better solution.)

The following sections will help you ensure that they attend and will help you get results (i.e., new clients and more revenue for you).

Every day, there are thousands of potential clients and customers (brokerage houses call them clients; banks still call them customers) available to attend seminars. Some are professional seminar attendees, and some are individuals seeking satisfactory advice that they, thus far, have not been able to obtain.

A recent survey in 2005, conducted by an independent organization, should give you some insight into the motivations of potential clients and customers, indicating where you might want to focus:

Of high-net-worth clients ($500,000-plus), 58% now prefer smaller, independent, "conflict-free" brokerage houses. Of this group, issues relating to their needs and financial outlook were confidence and trust, customized solutions, professional designations and licenses, total financial management services, and open discussions about obtaining financial goals. Yes, 42% still favored large national firms, but they wanted the same things.

Surveys I have conducted (for current clients and seminar attendees) have made it clear that they like seeing an agenda for items of interest. Because they see an agenda and something sparked their interest, attendees at your seminars should provide better results because they have a specific reason to attend. They have also made it clear they like to know what your agenda is (i.e., Why are we here, and what are you going to offer that is different from anybody else?). So do your housekeeping up front!

Your goal should not necessarily be to do business right then and there at the seminar, but to entice an individual or group to set up an appointment later, at a time and place that is convenient for them to do business. I once tried a workshop for the sole purpose of conducting business—what a disaster that was! All I accomplished was to frustrate everyone, to run way over time (staying on schedule is very important to attendees!), and to conduct no business at all.

The seminar will set the stage for the subsequent interviews.

Let's look at what you need during an appointment with a potential client (What good are seminars and appointments, after all, if you can't close them?):

- A professional company book to hand out (chapter VIII). This does not have to be in color—black-and-white is fine—but it should contain the following:
  - A mission statement[1]
  - A marketing statement[2]

---

[1] Your mission statement should be short: "We provide investors with comprehensive, tax-aware wealth-management strategies."

[2] Your marketing statement should describe what you and your firm do for clients. For example, it might read, "We believe planning is a process: the more information we have, the stronger the relationship. One of the ways we start the process is to gather information; this allows us to develop a plan based on your short-term, intermediate-term, and long-term goals and objectives."

- A list of the information you'll need to collect from the prospective client, using the seminar workbook provided in this book
- Your personal bio and a profile of the company with which you are affiliated
- A list of the products and services provided by the company
- A description of how you get paid for your services (disclosure, disclosure, disclosure). 58% of affluent investors said they had higher trust in smaller firms. They also wanted customized solutions, professional designations for advisors, open discussions on how to achieve their goals, and realistic exit strategies for underperforming investments.
- A list of your referrals. (Always ask permission first.)
- Your web and e-mail addresses should match. There are plenty of places to obtain low-cost Web pages, such as www.bigstep.com. Or see www.netmechanic.com for search engine subscriptions.

Your professionalism in conducting an appointment will determine whether your seminar attendees become clients or not, so doing everything you can to prepare for a client meeting is crucial to your success. The clients I meet with have all made comments on how comfortable they are and how they appreciate the process I take them through. My typical approach to start the process is to discuss what has gone right or wrong with their investments and what they think they need to change. If you ask them about themselves, they will surely tell you. (It's a good practice to go back to your existing clients and review the seminar handout book with them as well.)

After our conversation, I consult my personal handout (shown later), which I gave everyone at the seminar and asked them to fill out before the first appointment. This gives me each prospective client's approximate portfolio values, account balances, annuity contracts, life insurance values, and summary of net worth (houses, property income, etc.). On the back of the handout, I ask for each of the aforementioned items (if your potential client brings the specifics, you know he or she is serious). After the potential client provides the requested information in the handout (including a risk-tolerance profile, brokerage accounts, bank, insurance, annuity contracts, etc.), I then ask for a time to set the next appointment. I let the potential client know that the second appointment is designed to help me review his or her financial needs and provide reasonable recommendations. On our third appointment, I present the proposal and any final changes and close the deal.

The number one concern I hear from clients is, "I don't want to lose any more money." I say to these potential clients at both the appointment and the seminar, "My motto is, 'If it isn't working, *fix it!*'"

Remember, individuals or groups attending your seminar are looking for you as much as you are looking for them. Keep in mind, however, that there are probably at least 300,000 financial advisors looking for them. In addition, the seminar is your one and only shot at impressing these prospective clients. So let's go back to the seminar itself and look at some important items and presentation skills that are essential to your success:

1. *Practice presenting.* Use video, mirrors, colleagues' feedback, or tape recorders. How you conduct yourself through body language, hand gestures, speech, and choice of topics is what makes or breaks your success. Stay away from irritating filler words such as "um," "OK," "absolutely," or "guaranteed." Do not look at the ceiling or the floor; talk to the entire group—not just one person—and avoid using a regular microphone with a stand (wireless microphones are the most professional).

2. *Get there early*, and make sure everything works: microphone, laptop, easel board, markers, and PowerPoint presentation.

3. Have a sign-in sheet and table (see chapter 5).

4. Have pens and paper (with your letterhead so it is your company name they see and take with them) for each attendee.

5. Provide evaluation forms at the end of the seminar (see chapter 10).

6. Print out your PowerPoint presentation, and have all your notes written on the presentation. (You should have it memorized). Make sure all your presenters have advance knowledge of your script, their roles, and your goals for the seminar so you are all on the same page.

The only thing worse than smelling like a goat *is to be the goat.*

Be Prepared, Be Professional, Be Effective!

Note: *You,* not the wholesaler, money manger, or guest speaker (the guest speaker is your attention getter), must establish the connection with prospective clients. So keep your speakers to time limits; *your strengths* should comprise the majority of the seminar.

Always do your housekeeping up front; let attendees know in advance what your objectives are. (See "the five steps of housekeeping up front" in chapter 7.)

III. The Power of Target Marketing

It is just as important to identify your target market as it is to prepare for a seminar or meeting.

Typically the seminar topics are designed for people with more money to invest; the type of questions raised by smaller investors alert the higher-networth investors of their presence, and the situation becomes uncomfortable.

Once you have established your market, look for database companies (such as Larkspur Data[3]) to help you specify your qualifications for a direct mailing. Generally, you can select direct mailings by state, ZIP code, city, or dollar amount and print your labels in any print type and size. I keep each client label list sorted by ZIP code for future mailings. Larkspur is accessible online, so you can change or expand your search fairly easily. Larkspur's prospect list is updated every quarter, so your client name base stays current.

Just because the prospects did not attend your seminar doesn't mean they are not still prospects! Design a "drip mailing" card on a 5" × 8" postcard. (Drip mailings are a great way to take a soft approach to let the individuals know what you offer, and help you keep your name in front of them, and newsletters are great here, too. I have provided an example later in this chapter.) I usually print 100 to 250 at a time at a print shop, so I can change my information all at once when I have multiple cards to mail. Add a quarterly newsletter; most companies have client-approved newsletters or compliance-approved ghost-written material to add to a newsletter. Or you can create your own (I use my own so I can control the topics), using publishing software, such as Microsoft Publisher. Once your compliance department approves it, submit the newsletter to the National Association of Securities Dealers (NASD[4]) for review. After an approximately ten-day review period (and $100), you can mail your newsletter. (The final approvals for changes from NASD may take thirty to sixty days, so don't print too many in advance.)

Newsletters are an effective way to communicate with potential and current clients. They are great image builders and offer a soft approach to your

---

[3] www.larkspurdata.com
[4] www.nasd.com

products and services. I make four pages of material on 8.5" × 11" pages and copy them onto both sides of 11" × 17" paper, which are then folded in half (this allows it to be regular postage stamp) for mailing. All the information on the front of the newsletter should make your readers want to open it and read more. Use the attention-getting phrase "INSIDE THIS ISSUE," and then cite your major topic so they can understand your journal's purpose without opening the newsletter. Keep information about all the products and services you offer on the back inside page, and keep the information neutral and not vendor-specific.

Sample 5" × 8" Drip Mailer

Multi-Strategy Portfolio Development

Trust & Investment Management

Annuities & Life Insurance

Wealth Management

Portfolio Review

Estate Planning

Bonds

XYZ Financial Company

555-1212
555-1234 fax

E-mail: xyzfinancial@investments.com
Web site: www.xyzfinancial.com

Always include your phone number, e-mail, and Web site address in the return address.

XYZ FINANCIAL COMPANY
FINANCIAL STREET
BIG CITY, USA 00000
555-1212
Web site: www.xyzfinancial.com
E-mail: xyzfinancial@investments.com

Use printed label for client address

IV. Market Your Target

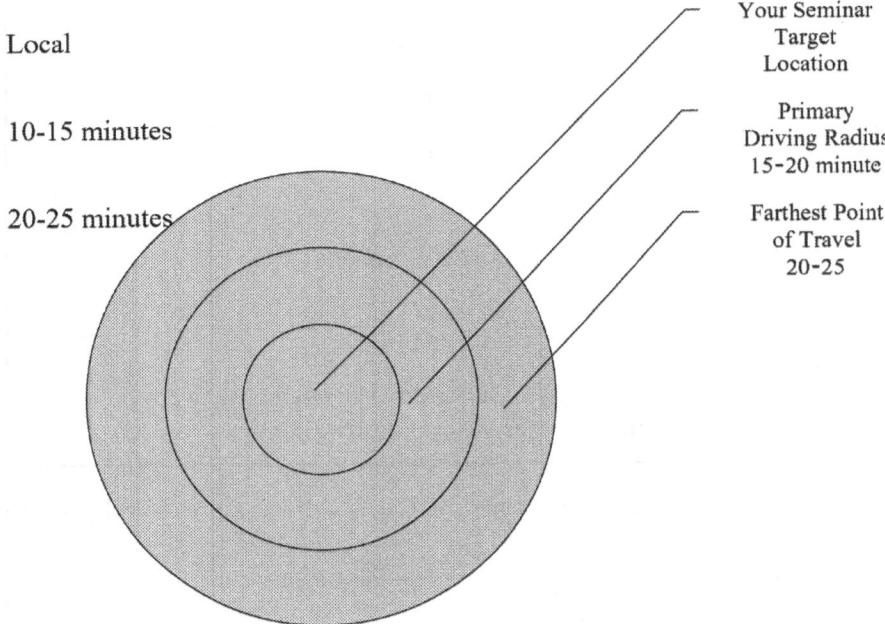

Local

10-15 minutes

20-25 minutes

Your Seminar
Target
Location

Primary
Driving Radius
15-20 minute

Farthest Point
of Travel
20-25

Larkspur Data can tell you how many people in any given ZIP code fit your criteria (e-mail Larkspur the ZIP codes in the areas you plan on holding the seminar). If there are not enough possible attendees, you know to look in other areas.

Identify the ZIP codes for your mailing, using a map of the area you desire to mail to (it is easier to identify your driving distances when you can visually see the areas on the map). You can obtain bulk-rate permits or postage-paid permits to limit costs. My experience shows that most individuals will not travel more than fifteen to twenty-five minutes to a seminar. So, pick a central location that everybody can drive to within that time span. Also, pick a location that most people will be familiar with, and make sure the venue can accommodate small- to mid-size groups and that they provide easel boards, slide projector screens, microphone systems, and extension cords for laptops and projectors.

If your chosen location is a restaurant, negotiate a set price for dinner (all-inclusive), based on the final head count from the replies to your invitations. Advertising in newspapers for seminars is generally expensive and provides you no control over who or how many may show up. The *only* way to invite guests is by reservation only; there's nothing worse than waiting to see whether someone shows up. Give them a good agenda and interesting topics, and they will show up. Besides, most people like RSVP invitations; the gesture makes them feel special. You may want to e-mail and fax your RSVP invitations as well. On occasion, I invite some of my best clients and ask them to bring several guests, usually for two reasons: one is to offer them additional products they may be interested investing in, and the other is that it creates a comfort level for the referral; the guests can make up their own minds.

V. Topics and Agenda

The next thing to consider is the agenda on the mailer; potential attendees will decide very quickly whether or not it interests them. Both clients and seminar attendees' responses have informed me they like to see an agenda; they show up because of something on the agenda they want to hear about.

I have found that 5" × 8"[5] ivory cardstock with the agenda posted (See next page) on it works just as well as expensive printing or stuffing envelopes (I've tried it all). I use black ink with the ivory cardstock; the cardstock stands out in piles of mail, they don't have to open anything, and can see in a glance the agenda for items that interest them. The most important element of your mailer is the opening line. People will read it first, and if it interests them, they read the rest.

So have an agenda of good topics and guest speakers, with at least one "hot" topic, such as "meet the portfolio manager from XYZ hedge fund," or "the bond guru." Limit your guest speakers' time to around twenty to twenty-five minutes each. The total program should only run about two hours.

---

[5] Copy the invitation so two will fit on 8.5" × 11" paper, and take it to a print shop. If you need 5,000, only print 2,500 and have the print shop cut them in half; the same for the other side for the return address.

BY INVITATION ONLY......*Seating is limited*

Presenting: John Doe
Director of Marketing, Wealth Management Group

Thursday, March 15, 2005
7:00 to 9:00 PM

Fancy Restaurant, Pastry Ave., Big City, USA
(Dinner will be served: call 111-2222 for directions)

AGENDA
Hedge Fund Investing
Direct Ownership Real Estate Trusts
Multiple Portfolio Strategies
Mutual Fund Investing Today

Sponsored by XYZ Financial Company

RSVP ONLY
XYZ Financial Company
555-1212 FAX: 555-1234
E-mail: xyzfinancial@investments.com

Return address side (individuals like to see all of this information on both sides):

XYZ FINANCIAL
One Financial Street
Big City, USA 00000
555-1212
555-1234 fax
Web site: xyzfinancial.com
E-mail: xyzfinancial@investments.com

To advertise the seminar, I normally do a 3,500- to 5,000-piece mailing to high-net-worth clients ($500,000 or more investable assets) and net about 20 to 30 + combined seminar attendees (generally a combination of husbands and wives) almost every time. You may need to send out more invitations, depending on the population of your target cities and towns. My goal was smaller groups that are more interactive and intimate: 20 to 30 individuals (or a combination of couples and individuals) gives you potentially 12 to 15 selling units. You will want to present to both the husband and the wife because they will both weigh in on financial decisions.

The best times for seminars are Tuesdays or Thursdays (Thursday being the best) from 7:00 PM to 9:00 PM. Leave ten to fifteen minutes for a question-and-answer session and the evaluation form at the end.

Feed them while you present. (I have tried having dinner served before the presentation: you run out of time. If dinner is served afterward, nobody stays, or they fall asleep.) I offer two choices of dishes (chicken or fish), coffee, and dessert.

Mail about ten to fourteen days in advance of your seminar (i.e., if your seminar is the 25th of the month, mail your invitations on the 15th); I used to do two seminars per week, one on Tuesday and one on Thursday to catch any overflow; I used to fill both days. I have been mailing into the same ZIP codes for years, with very few repeat attendees. The reason for some of the repeats was because the topic had changed. I always try to create a new agenda with a hot topic and an exciting guest speaker. If you provide advance notice, some of the wholesalers or companies you deal with can provide some high-profile guest speakers.

Note: Prospective clients only remember you and your seminar for 24 to 48 hours. So immediate contact is essential, with a phone call the next day or, as per the evaluation request, a thank-you letter to everyone who attended.

Have a call-in registry sheet for RSVP responses.[6] Ask for the name, address, and phone number of each attendee and the number of attendees per group. Ask if they want to bring guests.

XYZ Financial Company Wealth Management & Estate Planning Seminar Registration

NAME	ADDRESS	PHONE NUMBER

Remember to call the prospective clients the day before the seminar to remind them to attend!

---

[6] Use for the call-in and the seminar sign-in sheet

VI. Guess Who's Buying Dinner?

How do you pay for all this good stuff? Wholesalers, annuity companies, life insurance companies, and money managers can supplement your expenses. Be prepared to pay for everything up front; the suppliers generally reimburse you when you provide a list of attendees, cost of mailing, postage, and dinner receipts. Most wholesalers like to pay for seminar dinners with a credit card; the rest takes up to six weeks to reimburse. The rule of thumb is that for every $1 million in business you conduct, you get approximately 1% for seminar budgets. Assistance is conditional, based on the development of your business growth, but if you fail to reciprocate with business, the funding will stop.

When I do a seminar (once per quarter, some do seminars every month), I try to keep costs under $4,000, including dinner. You must be consistent and persistent; as you prepare for your next seminar, the results are probably just coming in from your last seminar!

To trim expenses, I go to a print shop with artwork I did on my computer and have them print and cut for me. For 5,000 mailers, I only pay for 2,500 pieces. (I make two invitations on one piece of 8.5" × 11" paper and cut it in half.) Postage is your next biggest expense. You can get a bulk-postage permit from the post office to cut the expense, and labels are fairly inexpensive.

The names of potential clients cost around 10 to 12 cents each or less, depending on the volume you purchase and whether your mailing-list broker is having any specials. So far, Larkspur is the only company I've found that provides viable higher-net-worth clients. Larkspur will provide you with information about the number of individuals that meet your qualifications per ZIP code. This allows you to plan your target areas more effectively. I like buying the list for control and sorting by wealth ability, location, and future drip/newsletter mailings and seminar mailings. Larkspur updates its lists every quarter, so they're always fresh.

I never serve alcohol at my seminars: it increases the cost too much, and I don't want the liability.

What follows is a sample seminar expense sheet. You should label and file every seminar for that date.

Seminar Expense Form

Seminar date:

Postage: _____ Printing: _____ Copies: _____

Labels: _____ Mailing List: _____ Rentals (laptop, projector, etc.): ____

Restaurant: Number attended:_____@$_____= _____

Company sponsors: Contributions:

_____   _____

_____   _____

_____   _____

Total seminar expense: $_____
Notes:

VII. During and After

As you begin the process of the seminar response system, you need to focus on your personal strengths, and your presentation skills. Focus on what you do best for clients, and stick to the schedule and agenda you set on your invitations.

As mentioned in the beginning of the book, take the five steps of housekeeping up front:

1. State your purpose
2. State your strengths
3. State your company's strengths
4. Let attendees know about the open question-and-answer period that will follow the seminar
5. Let them know about the evaluation form to be filled out at the end of the seminar (see chapter 10)

   At the end of the seminar, repeat steps 1 through 5.

As clients enter, greet them and ask them to sign in (see chapter 5). As you wait for other individuals to show up, mingle with everyone and create general conversation. You might ask, "What item of interest brought you here today?"

When you start your seminar, your opening statement should clearly articulate what you want to accomplish during the next two hours. (In addition to speaking to your audience, project your agenda on a screen.)

Here are some examples of how you might articulate your goals in your opening speech:

> Thank you for attending our seminar. We appreciate that you've taken valuable time out of your schedule to be here. Our goal tonight is to make you aware of the services our company has to offer, and we hope you will want to discuss this in further detail with us during a private, no-cost, no-obligation consultation.
>
> My job is to oversee the money managers, rebalance my clients' portfolios, and ensure diversification through proper product and service selections based on time frames, risk tolerance, and objectives. And as

a fun reward in honor of our guest speaker, we are going to have an estate (or whatever) quiz. The first correct responder gets an autographed copy of our speaker's book, *Plan Ahead: Protect Your Estate and Investments.*

We thank you for taking time out of your busy schedules to attend our seminar. We hope to get acquainted with each of you, and, when we are finished, I hope you will want to set up an appointment to see whether we can continue to the next step. At the end of the session, we will have a question-and-answer time. Please use the pens and paper provided to write down any questions, and afterwards we will hand out an evaluation form. We appreciate your honest feedback, and, of course, any appointments and topics (or topics we did not cover) you wish to discuss you may mark on the form.

We also have some literature you can take on your way out. (I usually do not give out the literature during the presentation, because attendees will read it and not listen to you.)

*   *   *

Thank you for attending our seminar today. As a free service today we are offering a free portfolio analysis. We have our company's information handout, which contains information we will need for an appointment, or just good information to help you succeed in your financial goals.

*   *   *

Welcome. Today we are going to discuss [quote agenda], and we hope you will like us enough to set up an appointment. To give you a little information about our philosophy, we do not believe in relative values; we set our benchmark at zero, and the second benchmark is you based on your risk profiles and expectations. What is relative value? If you set the benchmark at the S&P 500 and it is 20% down and the money manager is 16% down, he beat the benchmark. Unfortunately, he also lost 16% of your money plus collected his and the manager's fee. And does your current brokerage provide you with a comprehensive list of services (change slide to products and services offered) that our firm provides its clients? So the question you need to ask is, is the service worth the fee?

As a free service for attending our seminar, we are offering a no-cost, no-obligation review of your will or trust. You should have these reviewed every three to five years. Take advantage of this offer and mark it on your evaluation sheet.

*   *   *

Thank you for attending; we have a very tight schedule, as you can see by our agenda. If we haven't covered a topic of interest to you, please mark it on your evaluation sheet, and someone will contact you immediately, or, if we can, we will answer it during the question-and-answer session at the end of the seminar.

During your presentation, be direct, look at all participants (don't focus on just one), get approval from the crowd, and get their involvement (head-nodding, for example). Walk around (use a wireless microphone); don't stand and read from a podium. Use opening statements to get their attention: "How many have lost money in the last year?" "How many are sitting in cash?" "Wouldn't you like an investment that is stable in price and returns?"

PowerPoint presentations[7] with both open- and closed-ended questions and statements are the most effective. Sometimes you want a yes or no response, sometimes you want more, and sometimes you want to make a specific statement in response to a question.

If you don't have a laptop or projector, ask your sponsoring wholesalers whether they can provide one (most are more than happy to). Make sure you give your sponsor advance notice.

Use the PowerPoint presentation for bullet-point reminders, not for reading word-for-word, line-by-line (ugh!). Be interactive with the crowd (e.g., if you are on the 401(k) slide, you should ask, "How many people are still contributing to your 401(k)?" If nobody is because everybody's retired, then ask about rollovers.

---

[7] I have included several PowerPoint presentations throughout and in the "Effective PowerPoint Presentations" section. Make sure you get approval from your compliance department for all PowerPoint presentations and handouts before your seminar.

Use examples of thought-provoking questions on your slide:

> When was the…
>
> Last review of your financial plan?
>
> Last review of your wills or trusts?
>
> Last review of your investment strategy?
>
> Last review of asset allocation, types of investments, insurance, annuities, and tax management?

Ask "How many people have a financial plan? How many actually review their plan?"

"How many people have a trust? Is it funded or unfunded?"

Ask beneficial questions of the audience, such as "How many people have annuities? How many bought them before 1995?" Anything before 1995 had no step-up in death benefit, fairly poor investment sections, and no CDSC charges (generally) remain. So you can benefit the client by talking about newer polices that may be more advantageous for them and their families: "We offer free annuity checkups as a thank-you for attending our seminar."

Whatever your opening comments are, *practice*. Make it believable, and make it sincere, as it sets the tone for the rest of the show!

Note: All of this must be approved by compliance (including your RSVP, drip mailers, and newsletters). The guest speakers generally will provide a compliance-approved script and use preapproved handout kits from companies. (I prefer to use my own handout, which I have included in the next chapter.) By keeping the presentation open to a question-and-answer format, it is easier to get through compliance because compliance cannot control questions and answers. The purpose of such sessions is to promote interaction with the audience. Just keep the questions and answers within the scope of regulation.

The final step: hold the seminars regularly. You can't expect to do just one and be successful. Do at least one per quarter.

Lead time can be long in getting the client to do business. The higher the net worth, generally, the longer the lead time. Once you get an appointment, ask the right questions, get the information, and earn the respect of your client by being thorough, complete, patient, and professional.

VIII. The Seminar Handout and Client Preparation Book

Rule 405 of the National Association of Securities Dealers (NASD): Know thy client.

The seminar handout is one of the most important tools you have (that and the evaluation form; everything else they will forget in 48 hours). When the client leaves the seminar, it is your name, company information, and book they are leaving with. Likewise, the handout provides you with necessary information about your client when they return it to you.

It is imperative that you provide a customized handout; the handout sets the stage for you and your company. The handout presents your name and the information and requirements you want the potential clients to leave with and gives them information they cannot obtain anywhere else.

This document provides you with the information you need to establish all the risk and investment profiles of the potential client, education for the prospect, and the requirements for your next meeting.

You need your clients' "DNA profiles" for investing. The more information you have, the better you understand their real investment decision-making process.

Your handout also separates you and your firm from the rest; it is information anybody can use to their benefit. Your potential clients will remember this about you.

Estate and Investment Workbook

XYZ
FINANCIAL
COMPANY

One Financial Street

Big City,   USA   00000
                   555-1212
                   555-1234   fax

Web site: www.xyzfinancial.com

E-mail: xyzfinancial@investments.com

THE PLANNING PROCESS

The most common mistake individuals and corporations make is to think that estate planning is designed for those in the later stages of life. The reality is that you can never begin developing an estate plan too soon.

The planning process is straightforward:

- Identify your life goals
- Review where you are in meeting these goals
- Set up a plan
- Implement your plan
- Review your plan annually

One of the first steps toward meeting your goals should be developing or reviewing your personal budget. By defining your normal expenses, charitable gifting plans, emergency funding, educational, and other expenses in relation to your current net income, we can help develop a good foundation for your financial plan.

Your plan should also include provisions for savings, your children's education, mortgage protection, income protection, asset protection, funds for retirement, and succession.

The primary purpose of this book is to help our company to understand and establish a guideline for you and your family. We want you to understand how certain investments work and how they are taxed. This approach educates you and directs you to a better understanding of how they may affect your life and help create your financial foundation. Organization and preparation are essential to a financial plan; be prepared and be informed!

We hope this information is helpful to you and that you want to make us part of your current and future plans.

"Plan your future, not the government's."

Marketing Statement

The consultation is free (to determine whether either of us wishes to continue), and our approach is a full-service advisory role that encompasses all phases of investments and estate planning for you and your family. We believe planning is a process, and the more information we have, the better informed you are, the stronger our relationship with you can be. One of the ways we start the process is by gathering information. This enables us to see the whole picture; it allows us to develop a plan that is based on your current asset level, your short-term, intermediate, and long-term goals, your objectives, and your risk tolerances. Once we have the information we'll need, we review the recommendations and start implementing the plan. That is just the beginning; we stay in contact with you by phone for updates, by quarterly and annual reviews. The annual review is one of the most important. It allows us to assess how much progress we have made in accomplishing your goals and objectives and to make any necessary changes or adjustments to the plan. Let's take a moment to show you the services we offer at XYZ Financial Company.

PRODUCTS and SERVICES

Financial Planning	Defined Contribution Plans
Portfolio Design	Credit Lines
Investments	Checking/Visa
Estate Planning	Trust Services
Insurance	Corporate Health Insurance
Mortgages: Commercial, Residential	Business Checking
1031 Real Estate Transfers	Private Life Insurance
Private Annuities	Annuities

We offer customized investment portfolios, trust design to fit your needs, risk evaluations and assessments, investment policies, portfolio analysis, and estate planning for all your personal and business needs.

We offer one-stop shopping for all your investment needs.

ESTATE-PLANNING CHECKLIST

- Wills and trusts, living wills, provisions for executor, guardians, benefi-ciaries, successors, trustees. (Wills and trusts should be reviewed every three to five years.)
- Safekeeping for children's birth certificates
- Life insurance for estate taxes and living expenses of surviving spouse
- A copy of your trust or will with all proper insurance policy numbers, brokerage accounts, bank accounts, annuities, any other investments deemed important, and a video, with your attorney
- Life insurance on children; this will guarantee insurability
- Long-term health care provisions, durable power of attorney
- Wills do not provide for incapacitation; your will becomes court appointed without proper health and investment proxies. (Wills only become effective after death.)
- Adequate homeowner's insurance
- Mortgage insurance
- Umbrella policy (for additional liability coverage)
- Stocks, bonds, and mutual funds. (If you and mutual funds own stock or bond certificates, put them in street name with a brokerage firm. The brokerage firm holds them in their account in your name.)
- Disability insurance (how much does it cover and for how long?)
- IRA or other qualified plans—make sure that they have proper benefi-ciaries (spouse, trusts, etc.)
- Out-of-state property: What are each states probate rules? You should place out-of-state property in a revocable living trust.
- Annuities, investments
- Safe-deposit box, to include copies of Social Security numbers and birth certificates
- Business succession planning/key-man insurance, buy-sell agreements, specification of who takes over in the event of your death
- Current budget (review annually)
- Filing system that identifies all categories (auto, insurance, expenses, credit cards, investments, deeds to property, bank statements, taxes, etc.)

PERSONAL/BUSINESS INFORMATION

SECTION 1. PERSONAL/BUSINESS INFORMATION

Name: _____ *SS#/EIN#* ___-__-____

Home Address: _____

Home Phone: _____ Work: _____ Fax: _____

E-mail: _____ Work E-mail: _____

Occupation: _____ Employer: _____

Employer Address: _____

Date of Birth: _____ Citizenship: _____

Spouse: _____ SS# ____-___-_____

Spouse's Maiden Name: _____

Occupation: _____ Employer: _____

Employer Address: _____ Phone: _____ Fax: _____

Date of Birth: _____ Citizenship: _____

Children:

Name	Address	DOB SS#	Married	Children
_____	_____	_____	_____	_____
_____	_____	_____	_____	_____
_____	_____	_____	_____	_____
_____	_____	_____	_____	_____

You should make photocopies of every member of your family's Social Security numbers and birth certificates, and put them in a safe place.

Parents:

Name	Address	SS# DOB	State or Country born in* Name changes
_____	_____	_____	_____
_____	_____	_____	_____
_____	_____	_____	_____
_____	_____	_____	_____

*Helps in the establishment of the family tree, legacies, etc.

Grandchildren:

Name	Address	DOB	Parent
_____	_____	_____	_____
_____	_____	_____	_____
_____	_____	_____	_____
_____	_____	_____	_____

Great-Grandchildren:

Name	Address	DOB	Parent
_____	_____	_____	_____
_____	_____	_____	_____
_____	_____	_____	_____

PRIOR MARRIAGES:

Yours: _____

Spouse's: _____

Obligations to provide child support, continued life insurance, health insurance, or alimony for the benefit of prior spouse or children?

Living Will?   YES_____   NO_____

Provides health directive for life-support

Existing Will?   YES_____   NO_____

Last updated

Existing Trusts?   YES_____   NO_____

Are the trusts funded?

Inherited Assets:

Did you file 706, 1040, or 1041?

Value of inheritance $ _____

Federal Estate Taxes Paid $ _____

COMMENTS

_____

_____

_____

SECTION 2. ASSETS:

Market Value	Joint/Individual	Location/Acct #	Corp, FLP, Trust
Primary Residence	_____	_____	_____
Investment Real Estate	_____	_____	_____
Cash	_____	_____	_____
Stocks	_____	_____	_____
Bonds	_____	_____	_____
CDs	_____	_____	_____
Managed Portfolios	_____	_____	_____
Stock Options	_____	_____	_____
Annuities (Variable/Fixed)	_____	_____	_____
Life Insurance Cash Value	_____	_____	_____
Business Interests	_____	_____	_____
Managed Trusts	_____	_____	_____

Family Estate Trusts, Investment Management Trusts, Family Limited Partnerships, Charitable Remainder Trusts, Contract Trusts, etc.

Automobiles	_____	_____	_____
Jewelry, Art, Antiques	_____	_____	_____
Other Assets	_____	_____	_____

***Grand Total Assets*:** $_____

     Minus

Grand Total Liabilities (From Section 3: Debt)   –$_____

***Net Worth*:** $===============

SECTION 3. DEBT

	Balance	Loan #	Lender
Primary Residence			
Investment Real Estate			
Bank Loans			
Business Loans			
Credit Cards			
Automobile(s)			
Other			

SECTION 4. LIFE INSURANCE

	Policy 1	*Policy 2*	*Policy 3*
Type of Insurance			
Owner			
Face Value			
Cash Value			
Beneficiaries			
Insurance Company			
Loans			
Other			

Type of Insurance: Variable, Term (10, 15, 20, 30), Key-Man, Long-Term Care, Disability, etc.

Is insurance in a *trust,* or has it been *transferred* to a new owner for estate tax purposes? There are two things to remember about insurance: It is taxable at face value in your estate if you have any incidence of ownership, and gifting rules apply to transfers of cash values exceeding \$11,000 to new owners. Anything over that amount is subject to 55% gift tax *(reduced by 2010 to a top rate of 35%)*.

SECTION 5. ADMINISTRATION OF YOUR ESTATE

Definitions:

Executor/Executrix: The person or individual who takes your will to probate, collects the assets, orders appraisals, makes payments, and distributes the estate according to your will. *This individual is personally liable for the investments. Any beneficiary has the right to sue the executor for any losses in value. Make sure you make the executor aware of this fact.*

Trustee: The person or individual to whom the executor gives the assets in the event of minor children. The executor manages the money until the children reach attained age (most states are 18 years for attained age for children). The successor trustee is someone other than you or your spouse. The need for a successor trustee occurs in the event that both husband and wife die. While one or both of you are alive, you are the trustees. *Some states hold the trustees liable for any losses in portfolio values; any beneficiary has the right to sue that trustee for the losses. You may consider a corporate trustee for this service.*

Guardian: The person or individual who will take care of your children and make decisions on their behalf until they reach attained age. *If no appointment is made, the guardian could be the state.*

YOURSELF:

	Name	*Address*	*Relationship*
Executor:	_____	_____	_____
Trustee:	_____	_____	_____
Guardian:	_____	_____	_____

SPOUSE:

Executor:	_____	_____	_____
Trustee:	_____	_____	_____
Guardian:	_____	_____	_____

Please use the space below to provide any special instructions or requests for the aforementioned persons in the event of simultaneous deaths.

_____

_____

Power of Attorney-*Financial*   **Durable Power of Attorney-*Health Care***

Power of Attorney is necessary for deed transfers, etc.

Spouse: _____   _____

Other: _____   _____

If you or your spouse becomes incapacitated, the Power of Attorney may make health care and financial affairs decisions for you. Because you or your spouse are not dead, your will does not cover this. Instead, such power is court appointed.

SECTION 6. SPECIAL NEEDS AND CIRCUMSTANCES

You may wish to provide for your parents, children, grandchildren, and yourself[*].

Name	Address	Relationship	DOB
_____	_____	_____	_____
_____	_____	_____	_____
_____	_____	_____	_____
_____	_____	_____	_____
_____	_____		

[*]Long-Term Health Care Policies   _____

[*]Medicaid/Medicare Plan   _____

[*]QTIP Trusts (prior marriages for children)   _____

[*]Special Needs Trust   _____

List special needs requirements:

_____
_____
_____
_____
_____

Notes:

Asset Allocation Investment Cycle

As your life cycles evolve, your investment strategies will change. Financially, the life cycle progresses as follows: single, married, married with children, housing, college planning, investments, tax planning, retirement, estate planning, survivor protection, and income protection.

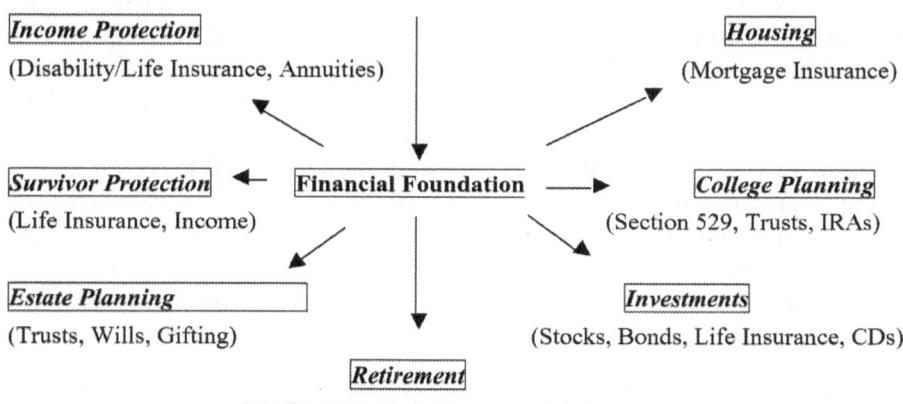

The following pages discuss the importance of understanding risk tolerance, investment options, the taxation of various investments, and how various investments work. Hindsight is a great teacher!

Prelude

Most of us have lived through the rumors: high earnings, high stock prices (*bull markets*); low earnings, low stock prices (*bear markets*); depressions, recessions, crashes; negative returns, positive returns; buy bonds, buy stocks, buy a mix of stocks and bonds; bad years, good years; analysts' expectations of growth; whisper numbers; market timing; dollar cost averaging; asset allocations; risk tolerance; time frames; and so on.

The following chapters are intended to give you insight on how to assess, calculate, and analyze investments and risk tolerances. Before you buy, understand what you are buying, the tax consequences of those purchases, and the risk factors involved with them. *After all, it is your money.*

Since 1926, the average return of corporate profits has run a pretty consistent 7.5%, and inflation has averaged around 3% for the same time frame. Charles

Dow formed the Dow Jones Industrial Average back in 1896. He assembled the top twelve or so stocks he felt represented the economic strength of America. We have split into other major components of the Dow, like the Transportation Index; the S&P (Standard & Poor's) 500; NASDAQ (which was founded in 1971 and consisted mostly of technology stocks); the NASDAQ 100 (symbol QQQ), which tracks the top 100 companies; Russell 2000, which measures small cap stocks (under $500 million in market capitalization); the Wilshire 5000, which is generally used to measure the total value of all U.S. stocks; and the Wilshire 4500, which measures small and mid-cap companies. The government tracks consumer spending (the Consumer Price Index [CPI]) for inflation. The CPI-U (U-urban) represents all consumer spending and accounts for over 80% of all households. Income tax brackets are adjusted to spare consumers from higher taxes based on inflation. Core CPI is used for longer-term inflation trends and tracks food and energy. CPI-W adjusts cost-of-living inflation and is primarily used to calculate Social Security increases. You can find more information on the Bureau of Labor Statistics Web site: http://www.bls.gov/cpi/home.htm.

The Securities Investor Protection Act of 1970 (SIPC) is the equivalent of bank SIPC Insurance. The general insurance coverage is for $400,000 or securities per customer of the Broker/Dealer, and $100,000 for cash. Government sponsorship is in the form of board appointments made by the president of the United States, the Federal Reserve Board, and the U.S. Treasury. Most Broker/Dealers have additional insurance to cover larger losses.

Basics to know to calculate your return on invested capital and to calculate ratio of price to earnings:

Current Return on Invested Capital:	Annual Dividend	2.20 =	5% return
	Current Stock Price	44.375	
Calculate Price-to-Earnings (P/E)	Current Stock Price	44.375 =	10 times
	EPS (earnings per share)	4.43	earnings

When you buy or sell a stock, it is referred to as T+3 (trade plus three days to settle), which indicates the amount of time you have in which to pay money due or to collect money from the sale. When companies pay dividends (generally on a quarterly basis), you can either take the cash or reinvest the dividend into the company stock. The record date on which you are entitled to receive the dividend is set by the board of the company; you must be a stock record-holder prior to that date. The ex-dividend date is generally two business days before the record date to be eligible for the dividend.

MUTUAL FUNDS

The majority of individuals are invested in mutual funds. It could be for college planning, 401(k) programs, or individual investing. Mutual funds primarily allow an economical way for modest investors (you may pay $10 per share for a fund and own several large corporations you may not be able to afford individually) to obtain the same professional advice and diversification of investments as the wealthy.

Mutual funds allow investors to pool their resources as shareholders in a fund, receive the investment advice of professional money managers, and share in the dividends, income, and gains (less expenses and fees) of the funds they invest in. The number of mutual funds today is staggering: more than 15,000. This is both good and bad: It allows for diversification, but it is very difficult and risky for the average investor. You should seek an advisor to analyze your risk tolerance, time frames, and objectives, to find the type of funds that may be appropriate for you.

The Securities and Exchange Commission (SEC), under the Investment Act of 1940, the Securities Act of 1933, and the Securities Exchange Act of 1934, regulates mutual funds. Mutual funds must be sold with a prospectus to each individual shareholder. The prospectus explains fees, investment objectives, and expenses, and it outlines commissions paid to broker by the buyer of the funds.

The operation of a mutual fund depends on the following parties:

Board of directors/trustees, officers, attorneys, independent public accountant, custodian, administrator, transfer agent, principal underwriter, investment advisor, and you, the shareholder.

Almost all funds are all externally managed; they generally have no employees and hire outside investment managers, broker-dealers, and banks.

There are three types of general class funds:

- Class A shares generally have an "up-front sales load (commission)" that ranges from 3.5% to 8.5%.
- Class B shares are no-load up-front (no commission) but have declining sales charges over a period of years from date of purchase.
- Class C shares generally have no load up-front (no commission) but have a declining sales charge if taken out (redemption) prior to owning the fund for at least one year. After a year, the charge is usually 1% of the purchase price.

Most mutual funds are open-ended funds, meaning they can be purchased or redeemed (just like stocks) at any time for current value. At the end of each year, they generally pay a capital gain, which is passed on to each shareholder. Most people do not redeem the gain but reinvest back into more shares of the fund at the NAV (Net Asset Value—if you paid $20 and it posted a $5 per share gain, the new NAV at which you purchased additional shares is $15). In retrospect, the fund share value could lose money, still post a profit, but pass on the loss to you as a shareholder (so you lose value and money and pay taxes).

When you receive your 1099B for capital gains, if you reinvest you pay the tax on that gain but receive no cash (you purchased more shares) and hope the value increases over the course of the year. Dividend reinvestment increases your number of shares. Each year mutual funds take a step-up in basis for redemption because you pay your tax each year on any gains. Variable annuities may offer some relief from capital gains because they grow tax deferred regardless of whether it is a qualified (IRA or 403(b) or 401(k) or non-qualified plans which people contribute after exhausting all the contributions to existing IRA's or defined contribution plans. Most of the same mutual funds are available with the annuity. They are sometimes called bleeder funds—a company buys the right to use funds from the fund company and micromanages the funds inside the annuity they sell. Qualified plans are attractive for mutual funds because of pretax dollars and tax-deferred growth on capital gains and dividends.

Thus accumulation of wealth over the long term, diversification, systematic investing, and dollar cost averaging are important strategies, but it is critical to pay attention to your money and where it goes and what it does.

Capital gains play an important role in buying and investment strategies. At the current rate, people in the 15% income tax bracket pay a 15% capital gains rate on their profit, 20% for all others after one year. If sold prior to one year, ordinary income tax is paid (which means if you are in the 37.6% bracket, you pay a 37.6% capital gains rate, so it makes you think about longer-term holding). *For 2006 and beyond, the income tax/short-term capital gains tax drops to 35%.*

Undistributed long-term gains from closed-end funds: Some closed-end funds elect to pay tax on the gains they realize at their own corporate tax rate and reinvest the proceeds back into the fund rather than distribute long-term capital gains to clients. If this is the case, you must file a separate Form 2439, Notice to Shareholder of Undistributed Long-Term Capital Gains. This is reported on line 64, page 2, of Form 1040. Copy B of the Form 2439 must be attached to your return. The cost basis is increased by the difference between long-term capital gains not distributed and the taxes paid by the fund.

BONDS

All bonds have similar characteristics. They represent the indebtedness (liability) of their issuers in return for a specified sum (principal). All debt has a maturity date that extends anywhere from one day to thirty years. Short-term debt is generally under one year to maturity, intermediate debt is one to ten years, and long-term debt is generally ten years or more. The bondholders receive a fixed interest rate (usually for the lifetime of the bond duration) called the coupon rate. The rate of return for the interest can be calculated in either of two ways: current yield, which is the annual flow of interest or income, or yield to maturity, which is the yield if the bond is held to maturity and redeemed at par (bond par value is $1,000) value. Each debt agreement has obligations that must be met. These are stated in the legal documents, which include date of maturity, coupon rate, pledges of collateral, and any other conditions that must be met. There are two types of bonds: *bearer bonds* (coupon bonds; anybody can cash them since there are no names on the bonds to identify ownership) and *registered bonds*; the bonds are issued in certificate form in the owner's name (held in street name if a brokerage account). All bonds carry ratings established by Moody's and Standard and Poor's. The ratings reflect the risk of owning the bonds (Standard & Poor's ratings: AA+, A, BBB+; Moody's ratings: Aa3, A1, A2, Ba2).

Bonds carry risk of default, price fluctuations (if interest rates rise, bond prices fall; if interest rates fall, bond prices rise), and risk of inflation (not keeping up with inflation versus interest received). Most bonds have a *call* feature that allows for redemption prior to maturity.

Municipal Bonds

- *General obligation municipal bonds* are secured in their principal and interest payments by the full faith, credit, and taxing power of the issuing state or local government.
- *Revenue bonds* are backed directly by the revenues of a particular project, such as a road or a bridge.

- *Insured municipals* offer a high degree of credit safety. If the issuer of the insured bonds defaults, an insurance company agrees to pay both principal and interest when they come due.
- *Prerefunded municipals* are for security; most of them are secured by U.S. government-guaranteed securities.
- *AMT municipals* have interest subject to the alternative minimum tax (AMT). Some AMT bonds offer higher tax-free yields to investors who do not have to pay AMT tax.
- *Zero coupon municipals* do not pay interest semiannually but are sold at deep discounts to their face value at maturity. You collect all the interest and principal at maturity.
- *Original issue discount (OID)* bonds give the original purchaser a tax-free capital gain if held to maturity. Selling prior to maturity at a profit gives the owner tax-free profit for the period held (accreting).

  Example: *You buy a ten-year OID maturity at $900 (bond par is $1,000). The bond is held for five years and sold at $960. The $60 profit is taxed as shown in the following illustration:*

  <u>$100 discount</u>

	10 years = $10 accreted interest
Profit	*$60*
$10 per year × 5 years held	*−$50*
Capital gain on sale	*$10*

  If sold below $950 (900 plus 50 accreted interest), it would be a deductible loss.

OID bonds require the owner to include ordinary income each year as a pro-rated portion of the discount earned (accreted) for the period held. You must file IRS Form 1099-OID, which indicates the amount to include in income. This adjusts the cost basis each year so that you are not taxed twice.

U.S. Treasuries offer the highest degree of creditworthiness, and timely payments of interest and principal are guaranteed by the full faith of the federal government. They include locked-in interest rates. Many corporate and municipal bonds contain call provisions that allow issuers to call them before maturity. When bonds are called after interest rates drop, investors lose the higher rate of return and must reinvest at the lower rate. Most treasuries, however, cannot be called or redeemed before their final maturity date.

Liquidity: U.S. Treasuries are the most liquid fixed income.

Selection is attractive to the secondary market because of the no-call feature.

Tax advantage: Interest is exempt from state and local taxes.

- *Treasury notes* are intermediate term, issued in one- to ten-year maturity rates from $1,000 to $100,000.

- *Treasury bonds* are long-term debt, mature in ten years or more, and are issued in denominations from $1,000 to $1 million.

- *Treasury bills* are sold in denominations of $1,000 to $1 million and mature in three to twelve months. They are sold at discount through treasury auctions. The bond goes to the highest bidder.

- *Collateralized Mortgage Obligations (CMOs)* are sold in $1,000 denominations and are backed by the broad diversification of several mortgage pools; this reduces risk of prepayment by homeowners. Maturity and yield are very difficult to calculate; the underlying pools are backed by a government agency and guarantee timeliness of payments and principal only. They receive the same ratings as other bonds or Government National Mortgage Association (GNMA) loans of higher quality.

- *Series EE* bonds are appreciation bonds, issued on a discount basis (50% of face value). They start at $50 face value. They pay no interest but increase in value until maturity. You can redeem them prior to maturity, and you can either declare an annual increase in the value of the bond as ordinary income each year or defer taxes until redemption.

- *Series HH* bonds are ten-year bonds issued in exchange for series E or EE bonds in denominations of $500, $1,000, $5,000, or $10,000. They are issued and redeemed at par, paying semiannual interest over the ten-year period. They are subject to federal income tax but not state or local tax.

- *Series I* started in 1998 and pays two rates of interest: one that changes with the rate of inflation and one that is fixed. They are sold at face value (a $100 bond will cost you $100), earn interest through maturity (thirty years), you pay federal tax but not state or local income tax.

- *Serial bonds* are bonds that are issued by a corporation to finance a specific use, such as equipment that is pledged as collateral.

- *Convertible bonds are* generally issued with lower interest rates, these bonds offer a conversion to common stock of the company. They carry longer maturity dates and are generally callable. If the bond is called, the owner must convert. For example, if the bond were $1,000 and the conversion were for $20 per share, you would receive 50 shares of common stock ($1,000 divided by $20 per share = 50 shares).

- *Convertible preferred stock bonds* are usually used in takeovers of corporations. The Internal Revenue Service has determined that, because this would be an exchange in securities, as opposed to a sale, there is no capital gains tax due. So the winning company generally issues or tenders convertible preferred stock with attractive yields to entice stockholders to exchange their shares.
- *Corporate bonds* are bonds that are generally callable, issued by companies (if they issue more stock it could dilute the ownership of existing shareholders); instead of borrowing from the bank, they borrow from the public. Bonds are senior and preferable to common stock for security of ownership.

Bond Swaps: One bond is sold, and the proceeds are used to buy another bond. An investor may sell a low-coupon bond at a loss for tax purposes and buy a similar discount bond with the proceeds, thus establishing a capital loss to offset the capital gains in other transactions.

Taxation of Bond Premiums: Investors may deduct the premium paid at the time of sale by adjusting the cost basis or by taking an annual deduction for the portion amortized each year over the life of the bond

Par Bonds: A bond purchased at par value will not have any capital gains due at maturity. If the bond is sold prior to maturity, any change in its value is taxable as a capital gain or loss, as with any other investment. If a bond is called, the call premium, if there is any, is taxable as a capital gain.

Premium Bonds: The amortization of the premium on a bond priced above par is not considered a capital loss. There would be a gain (or loss) if the bond were sold prior to maturity at a price above or below its amortized value.

Tax Loss and Swap Worksheet

Tax-loss swap is the simultaneous sale of one bond and the purchase of a second bond to offset liability from any short- or long-term capital gains. Up to $3,000 of losses against ordinary income can be deducted in any year and carried forward indefinitely. You must also abide by the wash sale rules. A wash occurs when a bond is sold at a loss and another bond is purchased that is substantially identical within sixty-one days (thirty days before and thirty days after the sale), and applies only to losses. Always check with your tax advisor on wash-rule sales.

Par Value	Description	Coupon	Maturity	Cusip #	Cost Basis
_____	_____	_____	_____	_____	_____
_____	_____	_____	_____	_____	_____

Settlement Date: _____/_____/_____

Swap summary:	Sell Side	Buy Side	Net Change
Par Value	_____	_____	_____
Annual Income	_____	_____	_____
Average Coupon	_____	_____	_____
Average Maturity	_____	_____	_____
Average Price	_____	_____	_____
Average Yield	_____	_____	_____
Principal Proceeds	_____	_____	_____
Total Tax Loss	_____		

Taxable Versus Tax Free: *Taxable Equivalent Yield Table*

	Tax-free Yield						
	3.50%	4.0%	4.50%	5.00%	5.50%	6.00%	6.50%
	Taxable Equivalent						
[*]15%	4.12%	4.71%	5.29%	5.88%	6.47%	7.06%	7.64%
28%	4.86%	5.56%	6.25%	6.94%	7.64%	8.33%	9.03%
31%	5.07%	5.80%	6.52%	7.25%	7.97%	8.70%	9.42%
36%	5.47%	6.25%	7.03%	7.81%	8.59%	9.38%	10.16%
39.60%	5.79%	6.62%	7.45%	8.28%	9.11%	9.93%	10.76%

[*]Federal income-tax bracket

How to calculate bond yield: Calculate the yield on a bond by dividing the amount of interest it will pay over the course of a year by the current price of the bond. You must look at yield versus coupon rate, because a bond can trade above or below par (face value). The higher the price, the lower the yield. $\dfrac{\$70 \text{ (annual interest)}}{\$1000 \text{ (current market price)}} = .070 = 7.0\% = \text{current yield}$

Risk-Tolerance Worksheet

What is your current allocation of investments?

Cash	_____%	Stock	_____%
Fixed Income	_____%	Annuities	_____%
CDs	_____%	International	_____%
Real Estate	_____%	Other	_____%

What is your involvement with the decision-making process of your invest-ments? _____

What is your experience with investments?

Stocks___ Bonds___ Mutual Funds____ Options____ Annuites____ CDs_____ REITs____

Using the following questions, let's see where your risk and reward tolerances lie:

1. Strongly disagree
2. Slightly disagree
3. Neutral
4. Slightly agree
5. Strongly agree

I am willing to accept greater price volatility in return for potentially higher long-term gains.   Circle 1 2 3 4 5

Generating a return that offsets the effects of inflation is very important to me.   Circle 1 2 3 4 5

I do not need current income from my investments.

Circle 1 2 3 4 5

My investment goals are long term (more than seven years).

Circle 1 2 3 4 5

I am generally a risk taker.

Circle 1 2 3 4 5

I am generally not a risk taker.

Circle 1 2 3 4 5

I am willing to bear an above-average level of risk, and can accept years of negative returns before seeing positive results.

Circle 1 2 3 4 5

I do not need to convert my investments into cash; I have enough liquid assets to meet my expenses.

Circle 1 2 3 4 5

If I invested $10,000 in a long-term investment six months ago, and its current value is now $8,500, I would probably keep the investment.

Circle 1 2 3 4 5

The higher the numbers you circled in your answers, the more risk you are willing to take. Most people fall within the following asset-allocation categories:

- *Conservative*: Safety of principal is my main objective. Minimal risk.
- *Conservative to Moderate*: Safety of principal is the primary objective, but growth of capital comes second.
- *Moderate*: Growth of capital and safety of principal are both important. Moderate risk is acceptable to increase capital appreciation.
- *Moderate to Aggressive*: Growth of capital is the primary objective; a secondary goal is safety of principal. A fair amount of risk is acceptable in order to take advantage of greater growth opportunities.
- *Aggressive*: Growth of capital is the primary objective. High risk is acceptable in seeking superior returns.

SUMMARY

Every client deserves individual and confidential services, because every client is unique.

- Service
- Ethics
- Reliability
- Value
- Integrity
- Contact
- Extraordinary product selection

We will need the following information for our next meeting:

This completed booklet, broker statements, bank statements, life insurance documents, annuity contracts, wills or trusts, mutual funds statements, and managed portfolio statements.

Be prepared to meet for approximately two hours.

CLIENT FOCUS...

Our only job is to help you succeed.

Financial Advisor

IX. Effective PowerPoint Presentations

My PowerPoint slides are designed to create interest, be flexible with topics tailored to the audience, and promote questions and comparisons to their current situations. It is up to you to design slides, your company's structure, and topics that match your expertise. Use the following examples as guidelines and tailor your presentation to your audience as you go. As an example, in slide 19 when you ask the question, is anybody contributing to their 401K plans? If no one in your audience is contributing, switch your presentation and questions to discuss rollovers instead.

I use Microsoft's PowerPoint software, so I can design my slides in any format that suits my tastes and needs.

I have developed these PowerPoint slides over the years, based on feedback from prospective clients. They requested more open-type formats (not canned or performance related) and a variety of topics. The slides are forward-thinking, ordered in a logical sequence, flow naturally, and cover almost every area of events.

I've found 90% of my clients through my seminars, using the process and PowerPoint slide presentation I have outlined throughout this book. Whether you're a seasoned pro, an intermediate, or a beginner, go back to the basics: be prepared, be professional, be effective!

Make sure all material is compliance-approved before presenting.

Good luck and good selling!

Frank J. Eberhart, CEP, RFC
www.efsgestateplanning.bigstep.com

I've included the notes next to the slides (and other noted items) to help the reader translate additional important attention-getting information. These are things I've found that keep my presentations lively and interesting, promote questions, and identify services that my seminar attendees may not be receiving at their current brokerage or bank. Readers will need to write in the script that fits for them.

Slide 1	Planning for Financial Success Wealth Preservation Risk Management Estate Planning *XYZ FINANCIAL COMPANY* WELCOME	This slide should be up when your audience arrives.
Slide 2	**Today's Agenda** <hr>John Doe, Director of Wealth Management • Alternative Investments • Tax-Aware Investing • Financial Planning • Retirement Planning • Estate Planning • New Tax Laws	The topics for discussion. I change the "hot topic" every seminar. Tailor the topics to your company's strengths.
Slide 3	**Client Focus** *Our only job is to help you succeed.* <hr> • *Service* • *Ethics* • *Reliability* • *Value* • *Integrity* • *Contact* • *Extraordinary product selection*	Every client deserves individual and confidential services, because every client is unique. That is why we offer one-stop shopping.

Slide 4	**Overview of Services** *for all your financial needs* - *Financial planning* - *Portfolio design* - *Investments* - *Estate planning* - *Insurance* - *Mortgages* - *Trust services* - *Business*	List the information that fits your business.
Slide 5	**The Investment Cycle** Income Protection Survivor Protection Housing Financial Foundation Estate Planning College Planning Retirement Investments	The investment cycle duplicates the life cycle; each phase requires planning, review, and change of strategies, from beginning through succession.
Slide 6	**Where Would You Like to Be?** *Have you been there and need to get back?* - Financial independence - Secure retirement - Secure children's education - Estate planning You need more than ever to have a plan and investment strategy in place.	What steps have you taken to help ensure this will happen? Do you have an exit strategy?

Slide 7	**The Financial Planning Process**	How many people have set financial goals? (I think you will find that not many do.)
	• Identify your life goals • Review where you are in meeting goals • Set up a plan • Implement your plan • Review your plan annually And if it's not working, change it.	
Slide 8	**When Was the Last…**	We have learned from the last three and a half years of market decline the importance of all of these items. How many people have a financial plan?
	• Review of your financial plan? • Review of your will or trust? • Review of your investment strategy? • Review of your asset allocation, types of investments, insurance, annuities, tax management?	
Slide 9	**Investment Management**	The last three and a half years have hopefully taught us a few things; we need multiple managers in one portfolio with auto-rebalancing, better diversification of investments. I'll let (guest speaker) talk more on this subject. Investment policies protect the investor, the broker, and the firm. Investment policies keep investment risk tolerance at the levels intended. All require ongoing due diligence, fiduciary responsibility, with ongoing performance monitors, which include quarterly statements and broker reviews. You, the clients, have access to all of the performance records, with online ability, telephone contacts, and e-mail. It's your money— know what it is doing.
	• Tax-aware portfolios • Investment policies • Income portfolios • Alternative investments • Tax/estate planning • Trust services • 401(k) plans, IRA • Life insurance, annuities *Let's talk about strategies for today and for the future …*	

Slide 10	**Fixed Income** Introducing… John Doe *Portfolio manager, fixed-income advisor services*	This can be one of your guest speakers. Most affluent clients want to hear about fixed-income. Rich people buy bonds to stay rich.
Slide 11	**Alternative Investments** • Who buys hedge funds? • What are they? • How do they work? • Are they right for me? • How many are there? • Are they safe? Volatile? Regulated? • What are the requirements?	I use hedge funds and other alternative investments for clients sitting with cash in their checking accounts. It is also a topic of high interest for high-net-worth families. It also makes a great topic for a guest speaker.
Slide 12	**And Why Would I Buy Them?** • Stability, capital preservation, targeted returns • They are a non-correlated investment vehicle outside traditional stocks, bonds, mutual funds • Generally they invest in areas traditional portfolio managers cannot	Hedge funds are not for everyone. If you don't understand what you are investing in, *don't do it.* They invest in long/short equity, equity hedging/arbitrage, fixed-income hedging, index arbitrage, interest rate arbitrage, merger arbitrage, convertible bond/warrant hedging, interest rate swaps, derivatives, margin, futures, short selling, etc. (You get the picture.)

Slide 13	**Safety? Risks? Downside?**	They are designed for long-term investing.
	• There are 8000+ hedge funds, regulated and nonregulated. Stay with funds that are SEC-registered. Wealthy individuals and pensions invest to help protect their money.	
	• Downside is the requirements are still high for the investment, visibility of the portfolio is usually none, and K-1 filings can delay your tax filings.	
Slide 14	**Hedge Funds**	
	• Contrary to popular belief, hedge funds have very low risk (not all) and low volatility. They look for targeted rate of returns net of all fees. They are looking for investments beyond stocks, bonds, and mutual funds.	They help reduce risk; they are a non-correlated asset.
	• Risks are liquidity, delays from K-1, and visibility of the investment	*Make sure your guest speakers support your position, and limit them to between twenty and twenty-five minutes.*
Slide 15	**REITs** **Real Estate Investment Trusts**	
	Two types of REITs:	Will Rogers said it best: "Buy land—they ain't makin' any more of it."
	• Publicly equity traded. Trades like a stock; volatile; liquid; sell just like a stock	With REITs, it's what you are putting on the land that makes it safe or not.
	• Direct ownership. Non-traded, closed-end fund; redeem like a mutual fund	Real estate has become the fourth asset class.

Slide 16	**Education** - UGMA/UTMA Unified Gift to Minors Act - 2503(b) or 2503(c) trusts - Education IRAs - Roth IRAs - Section 529: tax-free growth, tax-free distributions if used for higher education, 5 gifting to the maximum each state will allow per child - Control	Even with the new tax law changes for contributions, the 529 offers the most flexible options in dollars-in and tax-free dollars-out. It allows you to keep control (after attained age); IRS allows 30% of contribution removed from your taxable estate. It can affect state aide
Slide 17	**Retirement** - At what age would you like to retire? - Are your investments keeping up with you? - Early retirement and can't access your money? Rule 72t - Are you maximizing your retirement portfolio? - 401(k)/IRA/annuity/rollovers	Rule 72t-allows distribution of equal installments for a period of no less than five years, or at age 59 and a half, without incurring the 10% early withdrawal penalty; ordinary income tax applies. With early retirements and buyouts, this has become an issue.
Slide 18	**Where the Money Comes From** Income population 65 or older, Social Security administration 1998 - Earnings 31% - Company Pensions 20% - Investment Income 28% - Social Security 18% - Other 3%	Most of your retirement dollars will come from a combination of these sources. The better prepared you are, the more should come from investments instead of Social Security.

Slide19	**Contribution Summary for Individuals Still Working**	The single 401(k) is designed if you have no employees other than husband/wife.
	Year 401(k) (403(b) Simple IRA) Single 401(k)	
	2002 11,000 7,000 40,000 2003 12,000 8,000 40,000 2004 13,000 9,000 40,000 2005 14,000 10,000 40,000 2006 15,000 10,000 40,000	If many in audience are retired, talk about rollovers and consolidation.
	2006 make-up provision: employees over age 50 can contribute an additional 5000 per year. Employers are not required to match the catch-up.	401 and profit-sharing plans combined could contribute up to 42,000.
Slide 20	**Estate Planning**	
	Author Frank J. Eberhart, CEP, RFC *Plan Ahead: Protect Your Estate and Investments* • Available at Borders, Barnes & Noble, Wal-Mart, Amazon.com, Walden Books, Yahoo!, BAMM • "Must read" (Today's Books)! • "How to Better Create & Control Your Financial Foundation" (Groves Library) • "A highly recommended primer" (Midwest Book Review)	Just to add credibility. Add your own bio or profile of accomplishments.
Slide 21	**Objectives of Estate Planning**	
	• To ensure the efficient transfer of assets to intended heirs • To minimize shrinkage of your estate • To provide sufficient liquidity to cover estate tax and other expenses	Have we forgotten the objectives of estate planning?

Slide 22	**Famous People** Source: 1990 Longman Group USA, Inc.	Great slide to show the importance of estate planning.

	Gross	IRS	Estate Net	%lost
Elvis Presley	10,165,434	7,374,635	2,790,799	73%
JP Morgan	17,121,482	11,893,691	5,227,791	69%
John D. Rockefeller	26,905,182	17,124,988	9,780,197	64%
Alvin Ernst, CPA	12,642,431	7,124,112	5,517,319	56%
Marilyn Monroe	819,176	448,750	370,426	55%
Walt Disney	23,004,851	6,811,943	16,192,908	30%

Slide 23	**Transferring Wealth** Three ways to transfer assets at death: • By law (joint ownership) • By contract (trusts, life insurance, annuities) • By probate	Joint ownership transfers all property to the surviving spouse; if there is no A/B trust or other arraignments, it is all taxable in the surviving spouse's estate. Insurance is income tax-free (but is subject to estate tax, unless in a trust); probate is if you have a will or testamentary trust provision.

Slide 24	**Why Avoid Probate?** • Cost and delay in distribution of assets • Time • Privacy *Tools for minimizing probate* • Trusts • Beneficiary designations (insurance, annuities) • Joint titling (only delays the process)	Talk about any clients that have gone through or are still in probate. Bad states: Florida, California, New York If you own property out of state, make sure it is in a trust.

Slide 25

More Common Types of Trusts
A trust is a legal entity that holds assets for the benefit of another person. The trust's beneficiary, a trustee, administers the trust.

- Private Foundations
- Revocable and Amendable Living Trust (RLT)
- A/B Credit Shelter Trust
- Irrevocable Life Insurance Trust (ILIT)
- Qualified Terminal Interest Property Trust (QTIP)
- Charitable Remainder Trust (CRT)

How many people have a trust? Do you have a tax #? Are assets titled to the trust? Separate power of attorney? Healthcare proxy? Living will? A/B uses the joint unified credit for federal estate taxes. ILIT removes the insurance from your taxable estate. QTIP allows income to surviving spouse but not corpus (protects children and other beneficiaries). CRT is a great way to remove nonperforming assets from your estate and receive favorable tax treatment and income for life.

Slide 26

What Counts?

- Federal Estate Tax is the net amount of your estate
- Everything counts: life insurance not in trust, portfolios, retirement accounts, pensions, business interests, works of art, etc.
- The IRS taxes everything over the exclusion amount (next slide)

Capitalize on your free will/trust review. These side notes are generally aimed at the client, they are next to the slide, no slide then it is intended for the reader

Slide 27	**Estate Tax Law**	
	Year Exemption Estate/Gift Tax 2003 1,000,000 50% 2004 1,000,000 49% 2005 1,500,000 48% 2006 2,000,000 47% 2007 2,000,000 46% 2008 2,000,000 45% 2009 3,500,000 45% 2010 estate tax repealed 35% gift tax 2011 sunset provision goes into effect. Exclusion goes to 1 million, 55% tax, plus 5% surtax for estates of 10 million but not exceeding 17.184 million. We also have a carryover basis for capital gains tax, and states have imposed their own estate taxes.	Just what the slide says. No estate tax in 2010; however, the gift tax over $11,000 is subject to 35% tax (not including your $1 million lifetime gift tax exclusion).
	"Note": This is a side note for the reader. Stay away from "performance slides;" once you focus on performance instead of the services you offer, your chance of losing the client is far greater. Performance is evaluated constantly; if you miss the performance numbers you probably will be out. The number one complaint when clients have left: *service/contact; performance was last.*	Always remember to get compliance-approval first. Customize your slides to fit your company's business.
Slide 28	**How Do I Minimize the Tax?**	
	• A/B credit shelter trusts • Life insurance trusts • Charitable remainder trusts • Gifting • Private foundations • Give it to Wall Street	Always have a little humor.

Slide 29	Do We Still Need to Plan?	
	• The federal estate tax is only applicable in one year, 2010 • Gift tax still applies • State death taxes still apply • We need to provide liquidity for possible capital gains taxes, estate taxes, and income for surviving beneficiaries.	The point is that the current tax situation is only temporary. With two presidential elections and four congressional elections between now and 2010, who knows? Plan ahead for 2011 and beyond. Or check the current estate tax law.
Slide 30	**Summary** There is a lot of uncertainty in the markets, estate planning, tax-law changes, and investment strategies. You need to plan ahead and know your options and choices. *Be Prepared. Be Informed.* *Please fill out our evaluation form.*	Repeat steps one through five of your housekeeping checklist. Guide the audience through the evaluation forms and collect them as they leave.

Whatever your practice or product, make your PowerPoint presentation entertaining, educational, and thought provoking, in a style that is all your own.

X. Evaluation Form and Quiz

Within the evaluation form to be given at the completion of the seminar, I include an informative quiz.

EVALUATION FORM

XYZ FINANCIAL COMPANY   *SEMINAR EVALUATION*
                                        APPOINTMENT REGISTRATION

Seminar Date:

EVALUATION: *For each statement, circle the appropriate rating.*

- The subject matter was effectively presented.

  Disagree   Agree   Strongly Agree

- Visuals related well to seminar topics & discussions.

  Disagree   Agree   Strongly Agree

- Our objective in this seminar has been met.

  Disagree   Agree   Strongly Agree

- The facility for the seminar was satisfactory.

  Disagree   Agree   Strongly Agree

- What suggestions or recommendations do you wish to make concerning future seminars?

_____

_____

Please Print:

Your name: _____

Address: _____

Daytime Phone: _____ Evening Phone: _____

Fax: _____ E-Mail: _____

I (we) would like a no-cost, private consultation to discuss the following topics (please circle all desired):

Multiple Portfolio Strategies, Estate Planning, Portfolio Review, Trust Services/Trust-Will Review, 401(k)/Profit Sharing Plans, Corporate Health Insurance Plans, Business Lending, Insurance/Annuity Review, IRA/401(k) Rollovers, Section 529 College Planning, Mortgages.

Other:

Best time to be reached: _____

We would like to thank you for attending our information seminar. We sincerely hope that we have achieved our goals for the topics covered this evening.

Financial Advisor

Test Your Knowledge

1. Life insurance is:

1. Income tax-free
2. Income and federal estate tax-free
3. Federal estate tax-free
4. Taxable at face value for federal estate tax

2. What is the
unified credit for 2005?

1. 500,000
2. 675,000
3. 1,000,000
4. 1,500,000

3. What is the average
time frame for probate?

1. One month
2. Three months
3. Six months
4. Nine to twenty-four months

4. What is the maximum
amount you can gift
each year without paying
gift tax?

1. $10,000
2. $11,000
3. $25,000
4. $20,000

5. Which is true of a
Revocable Living Trust?

1. Provides tax relief
2. Avoids probate
3. Reduces capital gains tax
4. None of the above

6. Which of the following
can you place in:
a revocable trust?

1. IRAs, 401(k), pension plans
2. Stocks, bonds, mutual funds, annuities,
   personal assets, homes
3. 403(b), 457 plans
4. None of the above

7. Can you give away an
additional $1 million
without paying
gift tax?

1. Yes
2. No
3. None of the above

8. What is the maximum
Medicare will pay for
nursing home care?

1. 1 year
2. 6 months
3. 2 years
4. 100 days
5. None of the above

9. Which is true of
Medicare?

1. Covers 20 days at 100% only after
   immediate hospital stay
2. Covers 100% for 100 days after hospital stay
3. Pays 6 months at 50%
4. Pays nothing

10. If you become
incapacitated, does the
executor of your estate
by virtue of your will
have the right to...

1. Pay your bills?
2. Handle all of your affairs?
3. Order health directives?
4. None of the above

11. For 2005 on a net
$2 million estate with
no A/B trust, what is
the federal estate tax
due?

1. 60% of $1 million
2. 25% over $675,000
3. 40% of $2 million
4. 48% over $1.5 million

12. What are the taxes
due on $2 million estate
with A/B in place?

1. 50% of $1.5 million
2. 60% of $1 million
3. 40% of $2 million
4. Zero

13. If you have a
testamentary trust
provision, at death
are your assets...

1. Distributed directly from the trust to
   beneficiaries?
2. Transferred to the surviving spouse?
3. Sent to probate first then back to the trust?
4. None of the above

14. What did most states
pass into law
in 2002?

1. Their own estate tax laws
2. A gift tax law
3. Their own federal estate tax laws
4. None of the above

15. In 2011, what happens
to the federal estate
tax laws?

1. They expire completely
2. They revert to 2001 rules

If you think this was difficult, just think what your surviving heirs and benefi-
ciaries will be up against without proper planning!

Note: When using this type of approach, have something to give away when they answer the question correctly.

Answer key:

1) 1 & 4	*3) 3*	*5) 2*	*7) 1*	*9) 1*	*11) 4*	*13) 3*	*15) 2*
2) 4	*4) 2*	*6) 2*	*8) 4*	*10) 4*	*12) 4*	*14) 1*	

978-0-595-37164-8
0-595-37164-7